Basic Domestic Pet Library

Choosing the Perfect Cat
A Complete and Up-to-Date Guide

Approved by the A.S.P.C.A.

Dennis Kelsey-Wood

Published in association with T.F.H. Publications, Inc.,
the world's largest and most respected publisher of pet literature

Chelsea House Publishers
Philadelphia

Basic Domestic Pet Library

A Cat in the Family
Amphibians Today
Aquarium Beautiful
Choosing the Perfect Cat
Dog Obedience Training
Dogs: Selecting the Best Dog for You
Ferrets Today
Guppies Today
Hamsters Today
Housebreaking and Training Puppies
Iguanas in Your Home
Kingsnakes & Milk Snakes
Kittens Today
Lovebirds Today
Parakeets Today
Pot-bellied Pigs
Rabbits Today
Turtles Today

Publisher's Note: All of the photographs in this book have been coated with FOTOGLAZE™ finish, a special lamination that imparts a new dimension of colorful gloss to the photographs.

Reinforced Library Binding & Super-Highest Quality Boards

3 5 7 9 8 6 4 2

Library of Congress Cataloging-in-Publication Data

Kelsey-Wood, Dennis.
    Choosing the perfect cat : a complete and up-to-date guide /
Dennis & Eve Kelsey-Wood.
        p.   cm. -- (Basic domestic pet library)
    "Approved by the A.S.P.C.A."
    Includes index.
    ISBN 0-7910-4604-4 (hardcover)
    1. Cat breeds. 2. Cats--Selection.   I. Kelsey-Wood, Eve.
II. American Society for the Prevention of Cruelty to Animals.
III. Title. IV. Series.
SF442.K46 1997
636.8'081--dc21
                                                      97-4186
                                                      CIP

CATS
Selecting the Best Cat for You
A QUARTERLY

By Dennis & Eve Kelsey-Wood

yearBOOKS,INC.

Dr. Herbert R. Axelrod,
Founder & Chairman

Neal Pronek
Chief Editor

yearBOOKS are all photo composed, color separated and designed on Scitex equipment in Neptune, N.J. with the following staff:

DIGITAL PRE-PRESS

Michael L. Secord
Supervisor
Bernie Gaglia
Robert Onyrscuk
Jose Reyes

COMPUTER ART

Sherise Buhagiar
Patti Escabi
Sandra Taylor Gale
Pat Marotta
Candida Moreira
Joanne Muzyka

Advertising Sales

George Campbell
Chief
Amy Manning
Director

©yearBOOKS,Inc.
1 TFH Plaza
Neptune, N.J. 07753
Completely manufactured in
Neptune, N.J.
USA

Over 100 million families in the English-speaking world own cats. Why? Independent and capricious—even when lavished with their owners' loving attention—there might seem to be little to recommend them as pets. But the fact that you have purchased this book indicates the very reason why cats are so popular: their special character, as well as their gracefulness and beauty, makes them much sought after as pets.

As you contemplate which cat might be the right one for you, also consider whether *you* might be right for a cat. Even though cats are among the easiest-to-care-for pets, they have special needs that must be met if they are to thrive in your home. If you are committed to devoting a good number of years to your feline companion, then read on...and discover the fabulous world of cats. Longhaired cats and shorthaired cats, common cats and rare cats, *Cats*: *Selecting the Best Cat for You* presents them all and details the qualities that make each one special.

What are Quarterlies?

Because keeping cats as pets is growing at a rapid pace, information on their selection, care and breeding is vitally needed in the marketplace. Books, the usual way information of this sort is transmitted, can be too slow. Sometimes by the time a book is written and published, the material contained therein is a year or two old...and no new material has been added during that time. Only a book in a magazine form can bring breaking stories and current information. A magazine is streamlined in production, so we have adopted certain magazine publishing techniques in the creation of this Quarterly. Magazines also can be much cheaper than books because they are supported by advertising. To combine these assets into a great publication, we issued this Quarterly in both magazine and book format at different prices.

Two-month-old Singapura kitten.

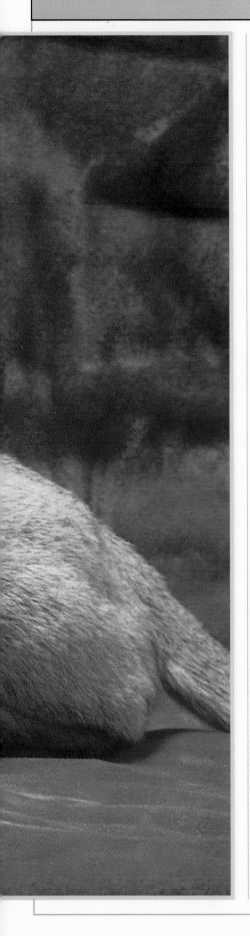

CONTENTS

Photography by Isabelle Francais.

WHICH PUREBREED IS FOR YOU?

The development of nearly all domesticated breeds of animals is a relatively recent happening. Although some breeds have existed for many centuries, the breeds we see today in cats, dogs, rabbits, and other pets were all developed within the last 200 years, many within the last century. The process of creating new breeds is, of course, an ongoing occurrence as there are always people striving, for various reasons, to establish a new breed.

When in discussion on the subject of breeds many people confuse a breed with a type or a group, therefore a definition is useful. Most dictionaries will define a breed; as a race, stock, sort, kind, variety or strain. Such definitions are far too loose because they embrace every possibility from, in zoological terms, what would constitute an entire family, or even a class, of animals to what genetically would be a group of essentially inbred animals.

We think a much better definition is given by The International Cat Association of the US (TICA) which seems to pinpoint quite nicely the essence of a breed. "A subpopulation of cats with respect to certain genetically determined characteristics which all members of the defined subpopulation share in common. These characteristics are described in the written standard of the breed."

The crucial words are 'written standard' for until this is appended to a subpopulation it leaves just too many aspects that would be contentious and would enable too many of a 'type' to be called a breed. This is especially true in cats which are all quite similar in many aspects, more so than in dogs, for example, where size and head shapes are so different. All the different breeds we see today developed from the various types of cats that were seen at any one point in time. This development has come about in basically three different ways.

Natural breeds are those cats which have been selectively bred from cats local to a region, a country, or even a continent. Such local types have been refined by breeding for uniformity of overall shape and maybe colors as well. Until enough people come together and draw up what all agree is the desired breed ideals, then the animals in that population may be broadly similar but they still cannot qualify as being a breed.

However, there is a gray area in this basis of a breed because it is quite possible that certain people may indeed have produced a number of

The American Shorthair is an example of a natural breed, which is a breed that has been selectively bred from cats local to a certain region, country, or even continent. Owned by Judith Thomas.

One of today's oldest breeds is the Persian, which descended from the long-coated Angoras of Turkey.

generations of a given type, that have become quite identifiable as a separate subpopulation without actually having a written standard. This can come about through geographic isolation or because the breeders are in a position to ensure the members of a subpopulation are isolated from the rest of the population.

We know of no present-day breed which has on either account been isolated for over 200 years in a clearly defined way such that present day breeders could justifiably claim that the bloodlines of present breeds have remained pure for this span of time. This would need recorded pedigrees and these just do not exist. Even if such pedigrees existed they would have little value unless they were accompanied by detailed descriptions of the animals featured in the pedigrees. However, many of today's oldest breeds will certainly be the shorthaired cats of Europe, the US and the Orient, together with the longhairs of places such as Persia.

The second oldest group of breeds are those which have come about as a result of a mutation. This will have given them some special feature which enabled them to be readily distinguished from most other cats in a population. It is possible that the longhaired cats actually fit into this category because it is by no means certain that these cats were developed from heavy coated wild felids such as the European wild cat, *Felis sylvestris*, as is often assumed. The tailless Manx is an old mutational breed as, no doubt, is the Siamese and maybe one or two other Asiatic breeds. A number of the Asiatic breeds have been developed from a type that has clearly been around for a long time.

The distinctive head and body shape of oriental cats stems from mutations that have been established for many centuries and have been spread by traders and travellers. When interesting color

The Manx is a mutational breed that originated on the Isle of Man, thus helping the isle gain recognition in the cat world.

The Himalayan is a hybrid breed that resulted when the two most popular cats of the world were bred: the Persian and the Siamese. Owned by Elizabeth Stamper.

mutations have appeared, these may well have been selectively bred for. These were spread to other nearby countries so that we arrive at a situation where numerous similar features are seen on cats, without these being fixed in any one subpopulation to justify the term 'breed' being applied.

The third group of breeds are those created by recombination of mutations. Obvious examples are the Colorpoint Persian, Himalayan, or Colorpoint Longhair, depending on which country you live in, or which registration body you support. Once a mutational form becomes well established then it is not long before breeders transfer it to other breeds

and thus create new ones. When the mutation is well established and there are sufficient cats in the subpopulation displaying that group of combined features, a standard can be prepared and then the subpopulation becomes a breed. Pedigrees become obligatory in order to retain the purity of the breed and some form of registration body is necessary to control these aspects. Until that point in time, it is a hybrid of the breeds that gave rise to it.

The whole subject of breed definition is very much related to the animal group you are considering. In dogs and horses color alone would be insufficient to raise those carrying a given color to the rank of breed, but in cats this is

possible. The term 'breed' is therefore dependent on just how precise the written standard is and where breeders, collectively, want to restrict variation in the breed.

Whereas a type can change as the years go by based on what new genes are introduced into the population, casually or intentionally, this cannot happen with a breed. Its standard clearly defines its broad characteristics, which can only widen or become more restricted by those involved in the breed altering the standard to accommodate changes. A breed's initial standard is usually loose enough to allow for the wide variation seen within those individuals which may be regarded as examples of the breed. As desired features become more fixed the standard will become changed to reflect this fact and to outlaw faults that have crept in along the line and were previously not mentioned in a standard.

BREED NAMES

The situation with regards to breed names in cats is somewhat confusing to the average person just entering the fancy. This is because the various ruling bodies do not work together to arrive at agreed policies or nomenclature. Cats are by no means unique in the matter, as it is a situation found in many animal hobbies. The problems arise when you read a book or magazine that was produced in a given country and is then sold in another without changes or notification of the names used in that country.

In this book if a breed is known by a differing name in the US and the UK then this fact is cited in the breed description chapters which follow. Fortunately, most breeds are known by the same name though they may have a different status. For example, in the US the Persian is a breed and all of the colors that are accepted are listed in the standard. In the UK, prior to 1988, the standard does not cite Persians, per se. They are called Longhaired cats and each color is given breed status. In June of 1988 the GCCF issued new standards and in this the Longhaired cats remain a section but the name Persian is reintroduced. The colors

remain as breeds of the Persian. Britain thus has many more 'breeds' than the US, being a matter of whether a given set of standards use color as a point of breed status or not.

COLOR TERMS

The names applied to a cat's color may change as you cross the Atlantic and when you change from breed to breed. The chocolate of the UK is called champagne in certain US breeds, while

Many shorthaired breeds have a counterpart that exhibits long hair, and the two are identified by different breed names. For example, the Abyssinian's (shown) longhaired counterpart is the Somali. Owned by Denise Ogle-Donahue and Kent Fleming.

lilac may be transposed in some standards to lavender or to platinum.

For the person who is simply looking for a pretty purebred kitten as a pet then all they need do is note the breed and the color. The potential exhibitors/ breeders then are advised to obtain the full set of standards from the appropriate registry they wish to join, and study these carefully so they are more attuned to the specific way a breed is classified and which colors are accepted at that

point in time. Colors are in fact being added steadily to many breeds and may be available in a breed even if the color is not at that time officially accepted in the breed standard.

COAT LENGTH

If cats of a shorthaired breed are also available with longhair, then this will be sufficient to change the breed's name. A longhaired Abyssinian is called a Somali, while a longhaired

Siamese is a Balinese. Each of these is a separate breed.

BREED POPULARITY

From the viewpoint of practical convenience the breeds in the following chapters are divided into either long or shorthaired. Certain breeds are actually a mixture of both, having long hair on their tails and some long hair in the coat. Such breeds will be found under the longhaired breeds in this book. While all of the popular breeds are available in North America, Great

Britain and Australia, there are other breeds which may be more restricted in availability. Generally, Americans will tend to recognize a breed much quicker than will the British, so some of the up and coming breeds may only be seen, in any sort of numbers, in the US or Canada.

What we were able to establish from the limited data available is that if the CFA figures prove to be typical of the US then it can be said quite certainly that longhaired breeds are much more popular in relation to the registered population of cats than they are in the UK. Some 78.4% of total US registrations are longhaired compared to only 40.3% in the UK. Conversely, whereas only 1.72% of US registrations are Burmese, this breed accounts for 15.5% of UK registrations. Likewise, the British as a nation obviously find the Siamese more appealing than do Americans, for the breed accounts for 24.8% of the total registrations, compared to only 6.1% of these in the US. The American figure also includes the Colorpoint Shorthairs, which have separate breed status in the US so were included in order to make comparisons more valid.

The second most popular breed in the cat world is the Siamese. The Siamese is known for being an intelligent and feisty breed.

SELECTING AND OBTAINING A CAT FOR YOU

If there are two groups of animals that can really sell themselves to you these will be kittens and puppies. This is even more true when young children are concerned and I doubt any parent has not heard the question, "Can we have a kitten, Mom?" Every year thousands of kittens are taken into households to satisfy the whim of a child and the end result is very often sad. After the kitten grows up a little, the child loses interest and the kitten becomes an uncared for stray, being replaced by the next unfortunate pet, be this a budgie, hamster, rabbit, or puppy.

Owning a kitten is a matter that should be taken seriously and no pet should ever be acquired for a child unless the parents want a kitten themselves. Cats are super pets but before they are taken into your home, you should consider their future. If you are one half of a married couple, does your partner share the same desire for a kitten? If he does not, then he will make the kitten's life miserable and it will become the source of arguments between you.

If you are purchasing a kitten for an elderly relative, remember that it might live for well over twenty years. What will happen to it should your relative die or have to be hospitalized for long periods? Answering these questions is called responsible pet ownership, and it is a sad reflection of our society that many cat owners should never have acquired the pets in the first

The Maine Coon is a muscular cat that is known for its independence. Its body structure stems from its wild ancestors that roamed the woods of New England to hunt. Owned by Susan E. Shaw.

place. The animal welfare organizations have the painful duty of destroying thousands of cats and dogs each year because they are unable to relocate the high numbers which are abandoned by neglectful owners.

If you are the sort who

The Persian is the most popular cat in the world. Persians must be groomed on a daily basis or their fur will become tangled and unmanageable.

cannot stand the thought of a cat jumping on your furniture or leaving a few hairs about, then you are recommended to consider another pet because you will not make a good cat owner. The ideal owners are those who do not place inanimate objects as being of more value than the welfare of a kitten, who are prepared to devote time to the grooming and feeding of the kitten, and who enjoy just having one or more cats about the home.

WHAT SORT OF KITTEN?
The fact that you are decided upon obtaining a kitten still leaves a number of queries for you. For example, you must consider what sort of kitten you want: color, breed, sex and whether you want it simply as a pet or if you have aspirations of showing or breeding. Take plenty of time to ponder these questions so that you make the right choice.

The choice in terms of colors and patterns is vast, and many of these are shown in this book, as are the numerous breeds and varieties of these. Both sexes are equally affectionate. The tom of course will spray his territory, including your home, unless he is neutered. This simple surgical operation is strongly recommended for all males unless you plan to breed them. It will also reduce his desire to

is performed on a female when she is between four and nine months of age and she is referred to as being spayed. The fact that a cat is fixed does not restrict its potential as a show cat, there are classes for both types.

PEDIGREE OR CROSSBREED

The question of whether you want a specific breed or mixed breed is really based on whether you have seen a cat

end up taking pity on some poor kitten or cat and decide to give it a home. This restricts the number of breeds we would otherwise like to own.

What you should ponder carefully is the length of the kitten's coat. A Persian or other longhaired cat may look beautiful in the photos in this book but that coat has received a great deal of attention. If it is not combed daily then it will quickly become a mass of tangles and mats. When the cat gets a soaking from a downpour of rain, it will come into the home looking a sorry state. This aspect should not be considered lightly or you may come to regret the decision. Of course, restricting the cat to indoors eliminates any such worry as well as other more dreadful dangers.

If you have any doubts on this then opt for a shorthaired cat because their coats require very little attention, or maybe one of the breeds which have some long fur, but not enough to cause too many problems for you. Many breeds today are available both as longhaired or shorthaired.

A purebred kitten will of course be much more costly than a mixed breed (moggy), and the latter can often be obtained at little or no cost. The fact that you do not have much money is thus no barrier to obtaining a beautiful kitten if you have a loving home to offer it.

The Selkirk Rex was derived from the crossing of a Devon Rex and an American Shorthair, which produced a breed with the typical rex-wavy hair and a cobby body.

wander and fight and will help keep the population of unwanted kittens down. The operation is best done when the kitten is about nine months old, by then his reproductive organs should be fully developed. Such a cat is termed a neuter.

The same is true of the female or queen but in her case the operation is of a more major nature, though still very safe. It will eliminate the probability of her presenting you with unwanted kittens. It

of a particular breed that you especially like. If not, then it is simply a case of selecting a kitten whose appearance appeals to you, and there will be no shortage of these. Some people cannot resist Siamese-like breeds, others fall in love with Persians, while others just love cats in any form and have a number of pretty ones that do not claim any particular lineage. Many of our cats are of the latter type, although we would love to own certain pedigreed breeds, we always

HOW MANY KITTENS?

Most first time cat owners will commence with a single kitten, and this is just fine, but really two would be a better decision. You will find that having two kittens will result in your having twice as much fun with them and two are no more of a problem to keep than one. They will spend much time playing together and will curl up with each other at night, both when they are kittens and very often when they are adults as well.

Two kittens brought up together will usually form a much stronger bond with each other than they will with others introduced to the household at a later date. If you plan to purchase a purebreed and your cash will not run to two, then why not have the latter as a moggy for it will be no less of a marvelous pet because it did not have a high price on its head. It is always very sad when a cat dies from an accident or other cause but if there are two or more cats in the household it really does ease some of the pain, for these still need your care and affection.

THE KITTEN'S AGE

The age at which a kitten should be purchased will be influenced by whether you simply want a pet or whether you are looking to become an exhibitor or breeder. If you are looking at the show world, you will need young adults because only at such an age will it be possible to really judge the quality of the cats.

However, if you have never owned cats before, then you should commence with a pet so you gain the pleasure and experience of bringing up a kitten. You may decide later not to show or breed, and if young adults have been purchased, you will have missed out on kittenhood, one of the nicest times of cat owning. You can still purchase what may develop into a fine show cat but should not be too disappointed if this does not turn out.

The best age to obtain a kitten is when it is about eight to ten weeks of age. At this time it is old enough to

From the creator of the Ragdoll comes this irresistible new breed, the Ragamuffin. Ann Baker, an acknowledged authority and breeding genius, knows what it takes to breed the ideal companion cat, and she's done it once again.

have been weaned but young enough to become fully socialized into your home. Not all breeders will agree with this age recommendation. Many feel that 12 to 16 weeks is preferable as such kittens will be more advanced and very well established, having spent a longer period with their mother. This, however, is not always an advantage from the viewpoint of socialization with human beings. Much depends on the attention the kitten has received from the breeder before you obtain it.

In just about every animal species studied, a hand-reared infant will make the most desirable pet, but removing such an infant from its parents places a tremendous responsibility on the person rearing the infant. In cats, such a situation is not recommended because the kitten will lose out on vital antibodies it receives from its mother's milk. Sometimes

The Pixie Bob is a new breed that was intended to possess a likeness to the North American Bobcat. Despite the wild look of the cat's face, the Pixie Bob is a trustworthy and devoted family pet.

The Ragdoll, is aptly named—its body goes limp when it is held. It is a slowly maturing cat that will not become full grown until about the age of four.

kittens are found abandoned when only about four to six weeks old, and it may be you who will acquire one of these. However, other than such circumstances, if you have a choice on the matter, then eight weeks should be the

The Exotic Shorthair, derived from a cross of the Persian and the American Shorthair, basically shows all of the Persian's characteristics except for the coat. Owned by Le Diagorn.

minimum age you should start with. Do not be offended if a breeder refuses to allow you to purchase their kittens at this age because their own views must be respected.

You should consider also the fact that in certain of the more rarely seen breeds you may have to reserve a kitten in advance. Do not assume that kittens are like commodity goods that can be purchased just when you decide is the time you want one!

WHERE TO PURCHASE

If your plan is to exhibit or breed the cats, then you will need to seek out a specialty breeder of the variety you want. It will be important that you know as much as possible about the line from which the cats come. By visiting a breeder you will be able to study the overall quality of their stock, which will be a fair guide to how your kitten will turn out. You may not be able to see the father of the kittens, for many breeders do not keep stud cats but use those of other breeders who have the capacity to accommodate entire males.

Before making a purchase, you are advised to visit a number of cat shows so that you can see what a quality cat of the breed you want looks like. At such an event you will also be able to make contact with breeders that may be in your locality and this can be useful at a later date. Maybe you will want another kitten from them or just someone handy to phone if you have a problem. Further, when you have your first litter they may be able to locate potential buyers for some of these because at that time they may

not have kittens of their own to sell.

Pet shops may stock both purebred and moggy type kittens and there are a few stores that specialize just in cats and cat products. Welfare organizations always have a selection of kittens that have been handed to them and maybe you could give one of these a loving home and in so doing save its life. Such places

A highly independent yet affectionate cat is the Turkish Van. The Turkish Van is sometimes called the "swimming cat," due to its attraction to water.

may charge a fee or simply ask you to make a donation.

Wherever you decide to obtain the kitten from, you should be sure it is from a source that is looking after its animals well. If the premises are dirty and clearly show evidence that the kittens are not properly cared for, then walk away. The last thing you want is to start out with a potentially ill kitty. In any case, people who cannot look after their charges properly should not be supported.

COST OF KITTENS

The price of a kitten can range from nothing for a mixed breed obtained from a friend or charity organization, through three or four digits for a quality purebred. If you only want a pet, then it is not essential that a purebred has to be of show potential. Very few kittens in the average litter will be of good show-quality (even though many breeders like to think they will be) and lesser-quality kittens can make nice pets.

You should be honest about such matters because you will not obtain breeding or show stock by telling the seller you want only a pet. If you ask for a pet that is what you will get. If you then decide to breed the results will not be favorable and you will lose out in the long run.

If you want quality stock then be prepared to pay for it. Your initial breeding will only be as good as the foundation females you start with. You may have to pay more for

The Balinese is identical to the Siamese except it has inherited a mutation for a long single coat. Owned by Ferenczi.

certain breeds than for others, depending on how popular the breed is in relation to the number of kittens being bred at that time. You may also have to travel some distance for certain breeds and this obviously puts the overall cost up.

A fairly new member to the cat world is the Munchkin, formerly known as the Creole Kangaroo, which developed through a mutation that produced basset-like legs. Scottish Fold Munchkin owned by Carol Higgins.

THE HEALTHY KITTEN

The singular most important consideration when purchasing any kitten is its health. This should outrank any other aspect. If you have obtained the kitten from a reputable source, then it should be in excellent health. If it then becomes ill, this will either be due to your own failings in providing for it, or as a result of its picking up an infection just prior to leaving the seller, or at any point thereafter.

For your own protection when purchasing a purebred cat, you should insist that it receives a veterinary inspection within 24 hours, and not later than 48, of your taking charge of it. Of course, you must expect to pay for the cost of this service. Failing this, you should take the kitten to a veterinarian as soon after you acquire it as you can. Even if your kitten costs little or nothing, it should receive a check-up

The Oriental Shorthair is best described as a Siamese possessing a coat color that is not accepted under the Siamese standard. Oriental Shorthairs possess the same body frame and personality as the Siamese.

because it may have fleas, ear mites, worms or other minor problems that the veterinarian can effectively treat.

The initial inspection should be based on watching the kitten's movements while it is playing. It should be lively and be running around without any impediment to its movement. A kitten that crouches in a corner is either very nervous, has been treated badly, has had little contact with humans, or is ill. Such a kitty is not for you, regardless of what the seller might try to tell you about it. You want a kitten with a bouncy outgoing personality that is totally confident in its little world. This indicates the seller has looked after it and spent time socializing it.

The next thing to do is lift the kitten up and give it a physical inspection. It should feel supple and well covered with flesh. Do make

allowance for the fact that many foreign breeds are not as stocky as domestic long or shorthaired breeds. If you are not familiar with these breeds, they can look as though they are in need of a good feed! The many photos in this book will give you an idea of what a cat of any given type should look like in terms of relative structure. The skin should be loose and you should run your hands all over the kitten's body to feel for any signs of lumps.

Inspect the toes and count these to see if the correct number are there and that they are well formed and soft to touch. The tail should contain no kinks in the majority of cats. A kink will not affect the general health of the kitten but would obviously be undesirable if you planned to exhibit or breed.

The kitten's breath should smell sweet and the teeth should be well aligned.

Again, in certain breeds the teeth have degenerated as a result of breeding for fashionable traits such as dished faces. In such breeds the teeth may not be aligned as well as they will be in a breed with a regular shaped head.

The eyes should be sparkling and free of any signs of weeping or staining, which would indicate a cold and possibly something more serious. The same is true of the nostrils, which should show no signs of congealed matter on or in them. The nose will be dry or possibly just damp but never cracked.

The ears should have no foul smell and no signs of brown or black dirt in them. The anal region should be clean with no signs of fecal staining, which could indicate any number of potential disorders.

One of the well-known blue cats is the Chartreux, who originated in France in the 1700s. They are gentle, mellow cats that enjoy human companionship. Owned by Eric Malbrecq.

The belly should be plump but not bloated. Inspect the fur and skin very carefully, especially in the longer coated kittens. You are looking for tiny specks of black or brown dirt which will indicate the presence of fleas or lice. You may see fleas scurry about as you part the fur. Fleas are brown or red in color, while the slow-moving lice are gray. The base of the neck, behind the ears, and the root of the tail are favored places for these creatures to congregate.

Any abrasions on the skin should be inspected carefully for signs of secondary infection by bacteria or fungi. Bare patches of skin, where there should be hair, are obvious signs of poor health. The hair of a healthy cat should have a high sheen to it and should spring back into place if it is brushed with your hand against its lie. However, a kitten will not have developed its longer, harder guard hairs so it will be both less springy and lustrous than that of an adult.

The kitten should pass each of these examinations and if it should fail on a minor point, then your option is to search elsewhere or to advise the seller that you like the cat but are a little concerned on the matters noted. A second inspection a few days later should see the problem resolved. Do not accept any kitten that is not in perfect health. If you are told a minor disorder will clear up quickly, then let it do so on the premises of the seller before you take the delivery.

When considering the health of a kitten do appreciate that certain breeds, such as the Manx or the Scottish

The Himalayan is so named because its coloration resembles that of the Himalayan rabbit. These cats are usually very quiet and are not extremely playful. Owned by Geri Hamilton.

Fold, are genetically abnormal. They may be associated with anatomical disorders that may not show themselves until the kitten matures. Generally, the first time kitten owner is recommended to stick with breeds that show no great deviation from the normal concept of a cat. The more exotic breeds are best only acquired when you have gained experience with cats, when you will be more attuned to any problems associated with them.

Likewise, if your choice is for a very popular breed, such as a Persian or Siamese, then it must be pointed out that the variation of quality within these will be far greater than within the lesser known breeds.

VACCINATIONS

Apart from a health check you can have your kitten vaccinated at about eight weeks of age. This will safe-guard it against the major feline diseases. Your veterinarian will advise you about the vaccinations. The breeder may also have wormed the kitten at about six weeks of age and their stock may have been tested for feline leukemia. However, in the latter case this does not guarantee your kitten is free of this so have your veterinarian test for it if this has not already been done by the seller.

The longhaired Manx, called the Cymric, was shunned by Manx breeders. Now considered a separate breed, the Cymric is an active, playful cat that has a lot of affection to give. Owned by Donna Chandler.

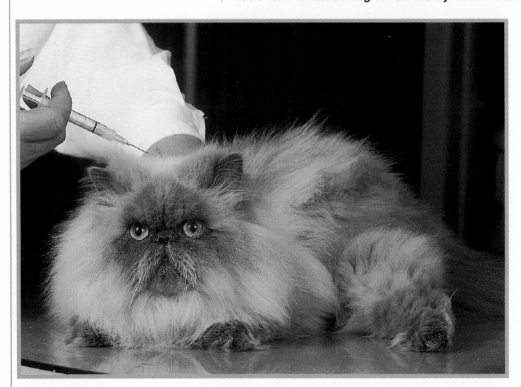

Your kitten should be vaccinated at around eight weeks of age and given booster vaccinations as needed. This will help ensure a long happy life for your cat.

LEARNING THE BREEDS

ABYSSINIAN

This breed was developed from imports made by British officers returning from campaigns in North Africa during the late 19th century. It is thought that the first Aby taken to Britain was called Zulu and that the date was 1868. By 1882 the breed had gained recognition but its name was changed to the British Ticked, as it was thought the breed was British in origin. This is most unlikely given the overall physique and the unique markings of the Abyssinian, which are very similar to those of *Felis chaus* and *Felis lybica*, two wild African species thought to be the original stock from which domestic cats were developed.

The ideal Abyssinian is a medium-sized cat that has a regal appearance and a lithe body. Owned by Denise Ogle-Donahue and Kent Fleming.

Ruddy, red and blue are the three accepted coat colors for the Abyssinian in the US—blue is the rarest of the three. Owned by Alyse Brissan.

The Abyssinian was the only agouti ticked breed of cat until the arrival of the Singapura. Each hair of the fur is a light color and on these are bands of darker color, with the tip being the darkest. Undesirable markings include bars on the legs, chest and tail, while an unbroken necklet is not permissible. Cats without markings on the underside are preferred.

In the US there are only three accepted colors and these are ruddy, red and blue. Ruddy is a burnt sienna ticked with dark brown, red is described as a warm glowing red and this is ticked with chocolate brown, and blue is a soft gray-blue ticked with slate blue.

The Abyssinian is a breed which enjoys plenty of garden or yard space in which to exercise. The breed is well suited to those who have ample time to devote to their

The eyes of the Abyssinian should be almond shaped, large, and quite expressive. Owned by Oliver H. Jones.

cats because this breed is very intelligent and will respond well to plenty of attention. If you are looking for a long established breed that is a little different then the Abyssinian may just be the cat for you.

AMERICAN CURL

The American Curl is another breed which is based on a simple dominant mutation. In this instance it is for varying degrees of curling of the ear, which turns outwards. The breed is not recognized by all American registries, nor by that of Great Britain and it is still being developed in terms of its type. This should be neither svelte nor cobby, so it is one of a number of breeds that is midway between the traditional European or American shorthair type and that of the Oriental breeds.

There is also a longhaired variety in which the coat should be medium long and silky—the shorthaired version having a shorter coat but also silky and lying close to the body. There appears to be no adverse side effects with the mutation, but the breed is still in its formative stage so it is perhaps too early to state categorically that this is so. It is an interesting breed but one that is unlikely to gain great popularity.

The American Curl should have a silky, semi-long coat with a minimal undercoat. This red classic tabby with white has a full-plume tail. Owned by Caroline Scott.

The name American Curl comes from the bend of the cat's ears, which must be at least a 90 degree arc, but never greater than 180 degrees. The brown-spotted tabby and the blue-eyed white are good examples of the different colors that may arise. Owned by Grace Ruga.

AMERICAN SHORTHAIR

This is America's equivalent to the British Shorthair from which it was developed. When the original settlers landed in the New World they took with them their cats and these became the typical street and farm cats of the US. They interbred with other street cats brought from other European countries and so they became every bit as American as the peoples who were forging this new nation. The result was a tough cat able to withstand the rigors of both the climatic differences and the hard times that most 'local' cats have to endure.

The first registered American Shorthairs were in fact British imports of the early 1900s but breeders quickly started to use American stock to increase the numbers of the breed. The basis of assessing the breed has not changed over the years so this remains a rugged yet beautiful and unaltered breed. Where it has changed is in terms of the colors and patterns, which are much improved when compared to your local street cat.

The American Shorthair is a medium to large breed with good muscle and a demeanor that suggests it is still more than capable of holding its own in the back alley! It is slightly longer than it is tall and the face is round and the cheeks well developed. The upper eye shape is like half an almond while the lower shape is one half of a circle. The legs are of medium length and powerful. There should be no movement towards either the cobbiness of the Persian nor the ranginess of the foreign breeds.

This silver tabby American Shorthair male exhibits the breed's well-developed chest and a large frame. Owned by Mary von Paulus and Valerie Anne Edwards.

The desired coat should be short, dense and hard, as would fit a breed that is capable of coping with both extremes of the temperature range. The density may vary regionally across the US according to the weather patterns. The range of colors in the breed is very extensive with the chocolate and the lilac being the two colors not permitted, while the only pattern not accepted is that of the Himalayan (Siamese).

You can not go far wrong if selecting this all American for it is both beautiful and hardy with no exaggerations to its form. It has an excellent personality that does not crave your attention all of the time, yet is very affectionate if given this. Its popularity as an exhibition cat has steadily increased and in its unpedigreed state it remains, deservedly, the most numerous breed in North America.

The head of the American Shorthair should be broad with well-developed cheeks, and the eyes and ears should be set well apart, as seen in this red tabby female. Owned by Mary von Paulus and Valerie Anne Edwards.

AMERICAN WIREHAIR

The Wirehair is an American Shorthair carrying one or a pair of mutated genes for hair type. In this case the hair is hooked and crumpled in the manner of sheep's wool. The original mutation appeared in Verona, New York in 1966. The breed is recognized by certain American registries but is not a breed accepted in Great Britain.

The hair should be springy, tight, and of medium length. The result is more of a ringlet than the formation of a wavy coat as seen in the rex breeds. The Wirehair is available in a wide range of colors and coat patterns but these do not include the Himalayan pattern nor the color choco-

The American Wirehair is a medium-sized cat that is energetic, playful, and has a lot of affection to give. Owned by Richard H. Gebhardt.

late or its dilution lavender (lilac). In order to establish type the allowable outcross is the American Shorthair.

In terms of its personality the Wirehair will be much like that of the American Shorthair. The mutation is transmitted as a simple autosomal dominant.

The unique texture of the American Wirehair's coat is due to the presence of all three hair types: down, awn, and guard. Owned by Richard H. Gebhardt.

Left: This tortoiseshell American Wirehair shows how the head is proportionate to the body. His round eyes and slightly rounded ears give the cat a harmonious appearance. Owned by Herb Zwecker.

BALINESE

This beautiful breed is a longhaired Siamese that first appeared as a mutation in the US during the 1950s. It was initially called a longhaired Siamese. It is has a lithe body with all of the features and personality of a Siamese, which are described in detail under that breed. It has been accepted as a breed for many years in the US but only in recent years did it obtain championship status in the UK. The coat is medium length and not dense so it is easy to cope with. If you like the personality of the Siamese but think they are too skinny then the Balinese will suit you because the long hair not only fills them out but also gives the overall lines a much softer appearance. Faults are the same as the Siamese.

In the UK and most American registries the listed colors include seal, chocolate, blue, lilac, red, cream, torties and tabbies. In the CFA only the first four colors named are allowed, while any other colors seen are classified as a separate breed known as the Javanese. In the US you are still allowed to use the Siamese as an outcross at this time, but this is subject to change. The eye color must be blue.

This is an elegant breed possessing the naughty charm typical of all Siamese type cats. It is well recommended.

Adult Balinese, seal point, and kitten. Owned by Gail Fine.

The Balinese is simply a longhaired Siamese, with the same structure and disposition. Owned by Ferenczi.

This Bengal kitten exhibits a desirable coat pattern, an expressive face and a loving personality. Bred by Andrew De Prisco and Barbara J. Andrews, this five-week-old kitten is out of Topspot's Simba.

broad modified wedge that has rounded contours, with large eyes that are set apart from each other. The Bengal can be either spotted or marble pattern in brown tabby, seal lynx point, seal sepia tabby, or seal mink tabby.

BENGAL

The Bengal first came into being in 1963, when a domesticated cat was crossed with a forest wild cat of Asia. The goal was to produce a cat that has the physical traits of a small forest wild cat, with the temperament of a domesticated house cat. The plan was to capture the colors and patterns that are seen in wild leopard cats by producing the original domesticated/wild hybrid. Along with the physical characteristics from the wild, the Bengal brings many hints of the wild into the home with its hunting- and stalking-type play.

The Bengal is a medium to large sized cat that has a feral look to it. Its hindquarters are seen to be slightly higher than the front shoulders, with muscular composition. The body is covered with a short to medium length coat that is thick to the touch. The head is a

Right: While the markings and color of the Bengal are of great importance to breeders, the cat's temperament and interest in people are equally vital for a true Bengal. Owned by Michael E. Nelson.

The Bengal reigns as the new king of the jungle, a hybrid of the Asian leopard cat and a domestic shorthair. Owned by Tina Woodworth and Karen Austin.

BIRMAN

The exact history of the Birman is not known other than it was developed in the high mountains of Burma and the immediate adjacent regions. Legend says that the breed was originally a white temple cat. One day a priest was praying when he was killed by an invading force. At the moment of his death his favored cat stood on him and stared at the face of the goddess who the priests worshipped. The cat's eyes turned a beautiful blue color while the body became golden—much more so at the body's extremities. However, the cat's paws rested on the priest and these remained white as a sign of the cat's purity. The next day all the temple cats had changed to this color.

The Birman first arrived in France during 1919 and it was called The Sacred Cat of Burma. It quickly became popular and breeders in Germany, as well as those of France, were instrumental in

The head of the Birman should be broad and round, with round-shaped eyes of a deep blue color. Owned by Paula Boroff.

improving the breed. It arrived in the US during 1959 and in the UK about 1965—surprisingly late given the short distance separating the two countries.

It is a well built cat, much heavier than the Balinese, and of good length. The face is round with ears of medium length. The fur is long without being excessive and there is a good ruff of fur around the neck. The tail is bushy.

It is quite possible that the Birman is of mixed ancestry with its original color coming from the Siamese. A mutation then introduced what is called white spotting to the paws and this is a variable feature in the breed, as it is in bicolored cats and other animal species. The long hair may have come from crossings involving the Persian. Certainly its ancestry is

The Birman was originally known as the Sacred Cat of Burma. It is a playful, energetic cat that at times can seem hyper.

very interesting and a good topic for debate but it is most unlikely that its true path of development will ever be known.

The Birman is a delightful breed being stockily built, available in a range of colors and with a nice personality to complete the package. The coat is silky and not difficult to manage, as long as it receives regular grooming. If you like the Birman then check out the Ragdoll as well.

This seal point male Birman shows the breed's characteristic white gloves and a long, silky coat. Owned by Paula Boroff.

BOMBAY

The Bombay is the hybrid of the Burmese and the black American Shorthair. The result is a black cat, which is neither cobby nor rangy. The head is nicely rounded and when seen in profile there is a definite stop where the forehead and nose come together. However, this should not appear pugged. The eye color is gold to vivid copper. The breed is not recognized by all American registries nor is it accepted as a breed in Great Britain.

Since the breed has still

The Bombay was originated as a hybrid of the Burmese and the American Shorthair, but its distinct features have earned the breed a following all its own. Owned by Herb Zwecker.

The Bombay should possess a round head without any flat planes, and large, round eyes that are set wide apart from each other. Owned by Herb Zwecker.

not been firmly established, outcrossing is permitted to the sable Burmese and the black American Shorthair. It will be some years before Bombay to Bombay becomes the only permissible mating. This is because until the body type is consistent it will not be possible to breed out the Burmese genes for color. It is an attractive breed with a nice personality. However, many cats are produced from mongrel random matings that look very similar to the Bombay so just how popular the breed will become is questionable.

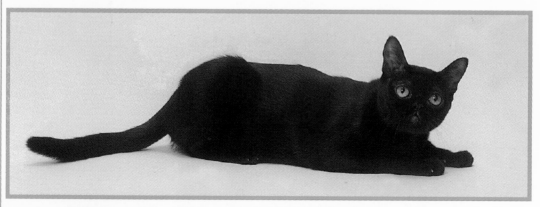

The Bombay should be black sable and must have a glossy looking coat. Owned by Karen C. West.

BRITISH SHORTHAIR

The origins of this breed go back as far as the first cats taken to Great Britain by the Romans. It is the street cat of the nation, albeit in a much refined form. The father of the cat fancy, Harrison Weir, was passionately fond of his British shorthairs and one of them won a first prize in the first ever cat show in 1871—of which he was the organizer.

The breed was pre-eminent in many of the early shows but slowly loss favor to the more exotic Eastern and oriental breeds which were being imported into England in ever increasing numbers. However, in more recent times the breed has enjoyed greater popularity as an exhibition breed, in much the same manner that the American Shorthair has in the US.

The British is a compact and powerful cat which must show good body muscle supported on strong medium sized legs. The head is round and set on a thick short neck. The nose is relatively short, straight and with a gentle stop into the forehead. The ears are small and rounded at their tip. The eyes are large and round. The tail is thick, of medium length and tapers slightly to a rounded tip. The coat is short, dense and crisp (hard) so it is able to withstand the rigors of the very unpredictable British weather, which ranges from sub-zero to very hot and from dry to extremely wet.

Just about every possible color and pattern of this is seen in the British Shorthair and these include the colorpoint (Himalayan or Siamese pattern) as well as the self chocolate and the dilution of this, the lilac. In fact we think that no other breed in the world is accepted in as many permutations as this breed. Especially famous are the British blue and the British spotted, both of which have been bred to an extremely high standard of excellence—but no British Shorthair can be a bad color if it is a good example of its type. In the US the Himalayan pattern, chocolate and lilac are not permitted in some associations, while a number

The shaded silver British Shorthair shows off the plush dense coat that is characteristic of this breed. Owned by Doane F. Huemmer.

of the other colors may not be available.

As with its American Shorthair equivalent, the breed retains all of the features you would classically think of as typical of cats. It is unpretentious, very beautiful, extremely hardy and is highly recommended—with or without a pedigree, depending on whether it is required simply as a pet or for breeding and exhibition.

This solid colored British Shorthair shows the well-rounded head with round eyes of a brilliant gold color. Owned by Kathie Prywitowski.

BURMESE

The Burmese is a very popular breed which is well established throughout the cat keeping world. It is neither cobby nor Siamese in type, yet obviously of foreign extract—this being the Siamese influence of years past. The original Burmese cat was an individual named Wong Mau which was imported into the US by a Dr. Joseph Thompson. This was a brown cat of foreign type acquired by Thompson during his travels in the Far East.

It was mated to a Siamese and from the resulting kittens, and a whole program of planned matings, the breed you see today is the result. It gained recognition in the US in 1936 and is accepted by all associations throughout the world.

It is a breed of medium size with good muscle that makes it heavier than it looks. The face is nicely rounded but in the UK is slightly more foreign in appearance than in the US.

The back is level from shoulders to tail and the legs are slim. The tail is of medium length and tapers very slightly to the tip. There must be no visible kinks in the tail. The ears are of medium size and rounded at their tips. The eyes are neither round nor oriental but should be an almond shape. The coat must be very short, satin-like and lay close to the body.

In the US only four colors are accepted in this breed but in Great Britain the list is much more extensive. The four basic colors are as follows:

Sable (Brown in the UK). Rich warm sable (seal) brown shading to a slightly lighter hue on the underparts. Champagne (Chocolate in the UK). A warm honey beige (warm milk chocolate) shading to a pale golden tan. Blue. A medium blue with warm fawn undertones shading to a lighter hue on the underparts (soft silver gray only slightly darker on the back and tail).

This sable male is showing off his muscular, compact body structure. Owned by Maureen Kramanak.

Platinum (Lilac in the UK). Pale silver gray shading to a lighter hue on the underparts (pale, delicate dove-grey with a slightly pinkish cast giving a faded effect). Additionally to these colors the UK accepts the following. Red, brown tortie, cream, blue tortie, chocolate tortie, and lilac tortie.

The personality of the Burmese is that of a very affectionate and highly intelligent cat. It is the sort of breed that thrives on company so is seen at its best when the owner has ample time to devote to it. As an example of its curiosity and intelligence a Burmese owned by one of the author's mother opened drawers in order to root about for things to play with. He was also observant enough to understand how to open the refrigerator door. This was discovered open one morning when choice food items were missing, and when this happened again it became obvious the door hadn't been left ajar by accident. He would also use the toilet to urinate in, so these really are very clever cats!

The head of the Burmese should be rounded without any flat planes. The face should look full with the eyes also being a round shape, the more brilliant the eyes the better. Owned by Maureen Kramanak.

CHARTREUX

The Chartreux is one of four breeds famed for their blue color. Its origins are in France where it is said to have been developed by an order of Carthusian monks who imported the original cats from South Africa. Others claim it is a cross between local French shorthairs and the British blue, or possibly with a blue breed known to have existed in parts of the Soviet Union. During the World War II, French catteries were badly depleted and at the end of the hostilities British blues were exported to France in order to help rebuild the breed, and maybe this is what has given rise to the British connection. In fact, a number of famous naturalists of the 18th century noted the blue cats of France whereas when a blue was exhibited in England during 1883 it caused quite a sensation. This would suggest it was a relatively new color to the

The Chartreux is seen only in the blue color, which may range from ash to slate. The coat should be unblemished and bright. Owned by Fred Andrews.

British who then gained world fame for the fact that they really developed the color to a very high standard. The Chartreux was first imported into the US in 1970 since French bloodlines have been used.

Whatever the history, this is a very attractive breed which is medium to large in size, cobby in build and with round eyes and a round face. The coat is medium-short and just slightly woolly, though enough so that its water repellent qualities are lost. The legs are of medium length, the bones being comparatively fine against the overall body mass. The eyes are copper to gold with deep orange preferred.

The color is any shade of blue-gray from ash to slate. The tips of the hair should be brushed with silver to give a distinct appearance to the coat. It is a hardy breed that

will appeal to those who like shorthaired cats and like them blue in color. As possible alternatives see British Blue, Russian Blue and Korat.

The Chartreux is a French breed that is agile and refined and can be very affectionate. Owned by E. Orca Starbuck.

The eye color of the Chartreux can range from gold to copper, but the preferred color is bright orange. The cat's alert personality should be expressed in his eyes. Owned by Suzanne Herhold.

CORNISH REX

The Cornish Rex is one of four mutations that have a similar effect on the coat. The guard, awn, and down hairs are variably reduced in length and become crooked. The Cornish mutation first appeared during 1950 in cats from the English county of that name. The coat becomes soft and wavy, the extent being variable. Although the standards in the US and the UK call for total lack of guard hairs these will, in fact, normally exist, but become so changed as to appear like awn or down fur. They are also greatly reduced in length. The breed gained recognition in the UK during 1967 and is

This smoke calico Cornish Rex shows off its fine-boned body and arched back that gives it a look resembling the Greyhound. Owned by Jessica Everhart.

now well established with all feline associations.

All of the rexes are lively and intelligent cats. You should bear in mind that their coats are not as water repellent as the normal coat so give them a brisk toweling, should they come in wet from the rain. The Cornish Rex mutation is transmitted as a normal autosomal recessive. If Cornish and Devon Rexes are mated then all of the offspring will exhibit normal shorthaired fur but will be carrying both of the rex mutations in a split or hidden manner. It is possible to obtain a 'double rex' but this would have no particular benefits.

The Cornish Rex is a curly-coated cat that is allowed in all colors. The chocolate and white bicolor is recognized and judged on the clarity of its markings. Owned by Babette Gray.

CYMRIC

The Cymric is a longhaired Manx in which the gene for long coat is thought to have been a natural mutation rather than having been introduced from any other breed. Other than its coat length it may be regarded as a Manx and you are therefore referred to that breed for a more detailed description. The breed was developed in the US and the use of a Welsh sounding name should not be taken to indicate the breed has any connection with that British country. The breed is not recognized in Britain, nor by all American registries.

The Cymric, like the Manx, is a breed based on a genetic abnormality—a fact that must be carefully considered when purchasing a kitten. Providing the kitten remains healthy and suffers no later problems, due to its genetic state, then it will make an interesting breed. The safer alternative to the breed

This red tortie Cymric shows the breed's typical round-shaped head. The head should be slightly longer than broad, with large round eyes. Owned by Donna Chandler.

would be the Japanese Bobtail, though these are never tailless and are not longhaired.

Notice the high rump on this tailless beauty— there is no penalty for a rise of bone or cartilage that may be seen on the rump.

DEVON REX

Devon is the county next to Cornwall in the West country of England and it is here that the second rex mutation occurred in 1960. It was originally thought to be the same mutation but matings with Cornish Rex cats produced only normal coated kittens proving the two mutations were at differing loci. Its original title was Rex 2 but this was dropped in favor of the present, more fitting name.

The Devon Rex is much the same as its Cornish neighbor but it does show a greater tendency to exhibit areas of much reduced coat, especially on its underbelly. This seems to be the result of certain hairs being more brittle and is possibly due to the effect of another gene action. The standards list this as a fault in a kitten and a serious fault in

This tortoiseshell Devon Rex displays a modified wedge-shaped head, with large, oval-shaped eyes that should be set well apart from each other. Owned by Ralph A. Covert.

an adult (as well as in the Cornish breed which does not suffer as badly in this respect). Select only kittens which show a good covering of hair. The availability of colors is the same as in the Cornish Rex, and the character of the breed is the same also.

The Devon Rex stands out in the cat world due to its unusual wavy fur that is short and full bodied. This fur has very distinctive texture that was caused by a mutation. Owned by Ralph A. Covert.

The body of a Devon Rex is long, slender, and medium sized, with a very hard muscular frame; as seen in this white Devon Rex. Owned by Don and Diane Moran.

EGYPTIAN MAU

Mau means cat in Egyptian and this breed was originally imported into Italy from Cairo. From here it was later exported to the US in the 1950s. After a breeding program was underway it started to gain championship acceptance with associations commencing in 1968. The origins of the breed are not known but it is regarded by those who are involved with it as the only naturally spotted domestic breed. Whether this is a genetic fact has not been established at this time. Regardless of this, the fact is, it is an interesting and attractive breed. It is not accepted as a breed at this time in the UK though various European registries do recognize it, as do all American associations.

The overall impression is of a mildly foreign type cat that is well muscled and of medium size. The eyes are

The Egyptian Mau is the only naturally spotted domestic breed. This silver Mau shows the contrast in coat color that the breed is known for. Owned by Kaye Chambers.

almond shaped and large; the ears are medium to large. The legs are of medium length and slender. The eye color is green, but an amber cast is acceptable in kittens and cats until maturity at about 18 months of age. The coat is short, dense and should exhibit a glossy sheen.

The Mau has a pleasant voice, is active, intelligent and easy to groom. Coupled with the spotting this all makes for a very nice breed that is likely to steadily gain in the number of people who own examples. When breeding, retain only the very best spotted kittens because this will increase your chances of stabilizing good spots in your particular line.

Right: The shape of the Egyptian Mau's head is a slightly rounded modified wedge with no flat planes present. The eyes should be large and almond shaped, and gooseberry green is the preferred color. Owned by Kaye Chambers.

Left: The Mau's graceful body and well-developed muscles complement its active lifestyle. Owned by Kaye Chambers.

EXOTIC SHORTHAIR

As with a number of breeds the Exotic Shorthair arose out of both controversy and the desire to change an existing breed. Many years ago a number of British Shorthair breeders decided to improve the breed's coat density by crossing with the Persian. The diehards in the breed were shocked at this and eventually the idea was dropped and any Persian influence was quickly removed.

The breed is thus a shorthaired Persian and, not surprisingly, the British standard closely follows that of the US (CFA) in all points. The main difference between the Exotic and the Persian is clearly in respect to the coat so the standard is quoted in respect of this, " Dense, plush, soft in texture, full of life. Standing out from the body due to density, not flat or close-lying. Medium in length, slightly longer than other shorthairs but not long enough to flow."

It is easy to care for and combines many of the virtues of the two breeds involved in its makeup. You will need to devote somewhat more time to grooming this breed, though it should never present any major problems. In reality coat length is influenced by the nature of other polygenes which affect the length of the other hair types (awn and down hairs), the thickness of these, their density, and their growing period. This enables a breed like the Exotic Shorthair to become a reality. Selection for both the required coat length and the density of this are important in order to arrive at a level of consistency in your litters with regard to coat length and texture.

The Exotic Shorthair is a breed of cat that is full of life—its body gives the impression of power. The body should be well balanced in form and almost round in shape.

This brown tabby with white Exotic Shorthair is showing the breed's large round head. The short neck is necessary to support the head adequately. Owned by Joann Miksa.

HAVANA BROWN

This breed is simply called the Havana in Great Britain where it differs considerably to the American version. In both instances the basis of the breed is the color which is

In the Havana Brown any vivid shade of green is acceptable for the eye color, but the deeper and stronger the color, the better. Owned by Richard and Lori Bilello.

described in the US as "A rich and even shade of warm brown throughout; color tends toward red-brown (mahogany) rather than black-brown. In the UK the color is 'rich warm chestnut brown.' Not dark or cold toned."

The breed originated in the UK during the 1950s when the color was specifically bred for. The initial matings included black shorthair to brown Siamese together with Russian Blue to Siamese. This clearly gave the breed a very svelte look and this body form was to be pursued by the British. Exports to the US were made, where crosses back to the Siamese were discontinued.

In the UK the Havana coat should be very short and fine in texture, whereas in the US it may be short to medium in length. In both countries it must be very glossy. If you live in Britain and would like the Havana in a lighter shade then it is called the foreign lilac and is created by the alternate mutant gene at the

The coat of the Havana Brown should be rich, warm brown or lilac and have a glossy sheen. Owned by Richard and Lori Bilello.

black locus. This lightens the brown of the brown mutation. In both the US and the UK the use of the Russian Blue during the development years will have introduced the dilution mutation and this will also produce a lilac color—it was originally called lavender.

The character of the Havana is very much that of a Siamese so it is lively, vocal, intelligent and mischievous. It will really depend on how much you like a deep brown color.

The Havana Brown is a medium-sized cat with a firm and muscular body. These cats are gentle and playful pets that enjoy the affection that you give to them. Owned by Richard and Lori Bilello.

HIMALAYAN

The Himalayan is a cross between the Persian and the Siamese and was developed concurrently in Great Britain and the US from as early as the 1920s. It gained recognition in Britain in 1955 and in 1957 in the US. Today most associations classify it as a color variation of the Persian to which it is indistinguishable in terms of its conformation (therefore see Persians for bodily detail). The term Himalayan is used in a number of pet species where it means the same as Siamese, that is, the

The head, like the one seen on this seal lynx point male, should be round, and broad with round, wide-set eyes. Owned by Vera St. John Pavlicka.

The Himalayan should resemble the Persian in coat length, conformation, and type. It should have a sweet look to its face and proportionate body parts.

animal's extremities (points) are of a darker color than the rest of the body. If they are not they cannot be called Himalayan without total disregard to the accepted meaning of the term.

In the UK this breed is known as the Colorpoint Longhair. When the breed is regarded as a color variant of the Persian this presents no contradiction in terms of

colors, because as long as the points are colored the criteria for the breed are met. An interesting situation arises where the breed is still classified as a Himalayan as in the ACFA. Here we see self colors listed in the non-pointed division of the breed, that is blue, black, chocolate and so on. Such cats, if they carry any Himalayan genes at all, can hardly be promoted as being Himalayan which would be akin to calling a blue or black cat Siamese!

As with all Himalayans the kittens are adorable and so easily sell themselves to you. In fairness to their future you must consider the grooming aspect. If you have the time to devote to this then it is a gentle breed that is not overly disposed to expend great energies running around. So it is well suited for the person who likes the quieter feline. The range of colors available is extensive and covers most of those seen in pointed cats.

These two Himalayans, blue cream and seal lynx point, show off two of the colors seen in this breed. Owned by Elizabeth Stamper.

JAPANESE BOBTAIL

The appellation Japanese was given to this breed because the early imports came from that country. It is not accepted as a breed in the UK but is recognized by all US registries, gaining initial acceptance about 1971. The basis of the breed is its short tail, which may grow to a variable length, but ideally should not exceed 7.5 cm (3 in). The tail should be covered with hair in a pom-pom style from its base and an area of flat lying fur on the tail is sufficient to disqualify or heavily penalize an exhibition cat.

In its appearance the Japanese Bobtail is of a foreign type with a wedge shaped head but is a more muscular cat than the Siamese. It is of medium height and the legs are long and slender. The coat is

The tail of the Japanese Bobtail should be upright when the cat is relaxed, and the hair on the tail should be slightly longer than the hair on the rest of the body. The head should have a triangular shape with gentle curves. Owned by Marilyn Knopp.

The Japanese Bobtail is a medium-sized cat with long clean lines and long bone structure. It is a well-muscled cat yet it should be slender, not massive in stature. Owner Marilyn Knopp.

short to medium in length and lays close to the body, having only a very moderate undercoat. It should be glossy and silky to the touch.

All colors are usually acceptable but certain patterns, such as pointed or agouti (Abyssinian) may not be. Bi-colors together with tri-colors seem especially popular.

This is a nice breed and although you might think a cat would look funny without a normal length tail it is surprising how quickly you get used to it and come to like it. You won't see too many bobtails about but their numbers have been rising steadily, rather than rapidly, over the last ten years.

JAVANESE

The Javanese is a longhaired Siamese in any accepted color other than seal, chocolate, blue or lilac. Put another way it is a Balinese in any color other than those already stated. The breed was developed from the Balinese but breeders in the latter breed were not happy to see non-traditional Siamese colors called Balinese, so it was decided to rename other colored cats of this breed Javanese. There is of course no connection between the breed and the Indonesian island of Java, nor between Bali and the Balinese as both breeds were developed in the US. The Javanese has no recognition in Britain or with all American registries, where this breed's colors are accepted as being Balinese.

This lilac-lynx-point Javanese shows the wedge-shaped head, which is in excellent proportion to the body of the cat, and almond-shaped blue eyes. The eyes of the Javanese should not appear crossed. Owned by Heather Kalt.

The ideal Javanese has a long tapering body that shows its lithe, muscular build. This blue-lynx-point Javanese is an excellent example. Owned by Heather Kalt.

The Javanese, like these lilac-points, are known to be highly intelligent, full of curiosity, and quite affectionate. Owned by Margaret Lowther.

KORAT

The Korat is an impressive animal which is blue in color. It is known to have existed for a few centuries in its native Thailand (formerly Siam until 1840) where it was especially popular in the Cao Nguyen Khorat district of east-central Thailand. It was first imported into the US about 1959 and gained recognition commencing in 1965. It was accepted as a breed in the UK in 1975.

To be able to register the breed you must be able to prove the kitten's ancestors were of Thai origin. In its homeland, where it is known as Si-Sawat, it is regarded as a good luck cat and often given as a present. It has never enjoyed great popularity and its numbers stay relatively low. However, breeders prefer this, for it means the standards in the breed are retained at a high level.

In appearance the Korat is neither cobby nor lithe and is a breed of medium size. Its face is heart-shaped and there is a slight stop at the nose where this goes gently into the forehead. The eyes are large and round when fully open—they appear big in relation to the size of the face. The coat should be short and very glossy. The desired eye color is a luminous green but an amber cast is acceptable. Kittens and young adults have yellow, yellow amber, or amber green coloration but this should be green by the time the cat is two or three years of age.

The color is a silver blue created by blue hair with silver tipping. The original cats, from which the Korat was developed, would have been black and a dilution gene

The Korat is only accepted in the blue color. It is a medium-sized breed with curved lines and a muscular, supple body frame.

The head of the Korat is heart-shaped with smooth, curved lines. The eyes are round when they are fully open, and when they are partially or fully closed they have an Asian slant.

would then have reduced this to blue. It is interesting to note that what may well have been a Korat was exhibited in England as long ago as 1896 but in spite of protests claiming the cat was a genuine breed from Thailand the judges of the day insisted it was a blue Siamese. The latter breed was as lithe at that time as it is today. The Korat is an interesting breed and will certainly appeal to those who adore shortcoated blue cats.

You will find that the blue coloration is subject to some variation in the breed so try to see a number of examples at cat shows before deciding who to purchase from. It is the extent of silver tipping to the fur that can change the shade.

MAINE COON

This is not a breed for apartments or confined living. It is a large all-American that likes the outdoors. The breed is thought to have developed from crossings between Angoras and shorthaired local street and farm cats. It was very popular at the turn of the century but slowly lost favor following the development of the more exotic Persians and Siamese breeds. However, dedicated enthusiasts kept it going and today its popularity is increasing. It has even gained preliminary status in Great Britain, so it is only a question of time before it has full championship status in the UK.

The origin of the Coon appellation to its name is obscure but it may be related to its fabled association with raccoons or to their colors. The Maine part of the name is for the eastern state of Maine where it was originally very popular.

It is a large cat which should have good bone and muscle as would befit a breed capable of looking after itself in the hard

The Maine Coon is known as America's native longhaired cat. It was originally developed as a working cat that had to be able to fend for itself in the woods under extreme weather conditions.

outdoors of America's far eastern states. While the coat is long it is not the woolly soft type but of a silky nature. This makes it easier to cope with, though it will require regular attention. There is a good ruff of fur on the neck, the tail is very profuse and plume-like and the hair on the sides is longer than that of the back. During the hot summer months this breed will shed much of its coat, but not that of the tail which retains

The Maine Coon is a large cat with a broad chest, good-sized bones, and long hard muscles. This red and white tabby shows large ears on a broad, modified wedge-shaped head. Owned by Betty Williams.

plume-like appearance.

You can have a Maine Coon in almost any color other than in pointed, chocolate or lilac, though there is no genetic reason why these colors cannot be produced in the breed and may well appear in due course. If you think you would like this breed then check out the Norwegian Forest breed, the Angora and the Siberian as they are similar in many ways.

The Maine Coon has a shorter coat on the shoulders that gradually becomes longer down the body. The tail should also have long flowing fur. Brown patch tabby with white owned by Colette Cowart.

MANX

The Manx or tailless cat is known world-wide amongst those with any sort of interest in cats. On the Isle of Man itself (which lies just off the English coast) the people are very proud of their tailless cats which have become a part of their history and appear on two of their postage stamps.

Kittens may grow to suffer from a number of disabilities of the spine and of the limbs

The Manx, known for taillessness, can have a slight rise of bone or cartilage over the rump. Owned by Donna Chandler.

appear today then it would gain no acceptance. It is recognized by all American associations.

In appearance it is a cobbily built cat of good size and well muscled. It might be described as a British Shorthair without a tail. The eyes are large and round. The rump of all cats will be higher than the shoulders but this is especially noticeable in the Manx. The tail, or lack of it, is crucial to the breed. There should be no evidence of a tail so the rump should be rounded with no rise of bone or cartilage interfering with this. Tailed Manx, of a sort, are possible and these are called rumpy-risers, stumpies or longies, depending on the extent of the tail. All colors and patterns are accepted in the breed with the exception of the Siamese pattern.

Above: The coat of the Manx should be short in length and have a soft look to it, as seen in this red tabby kitten. Owned by Donna Chandler.

Below: The head of the Manx is round and slightly longer than broad. Its eyes are large and round and its ears are wide at the base.

and the stilted action of this breed is the result of pelvic deformities. It does not follow that all kittens will suffer in any way, but potential owners of the breed should be aware when there are such obvious problems associated with a breed. It is only through historical acceptance that the Manx is recognized in Great Britain. Were the mutation to

MUNCHKIN

The Munchkin (formerly known as the Creole Kangaroo) is known for its short legs that occurred initially in Louisiana, due to a spontaneous autosomal mutation, that is a dominant gene mutation. The legs do not seem to prohibit the Munchkin from moving around effectively, the only difference is that they are unable to jump like normal cats do. Although the legs are disproportionate to the rest of the body, the other features are well-balanced. In fact, the body is moderately broad for having such stumpy legs. The fore legs are only slightly lower than the hind legs to give the appearance of a slight rise.

All colors are accepted, and the hair can be either long or short in this breed. The head is a modified wedge shape with rounded corners, medium in relation to the body. The Munchkin should have triangular-shaped ears that are moderately large, and large walnut-shaped eyes.

The Munchkin's legs do not hamper any mobility except jumping; their bodies must be well balanced and hard muscled. Breeders do not tolerate cats with soft muscles, sway backs, bowing of the legs, or any type of lameness. Owned by Laurie Bobskill.

The eye color has no relation to the color of the coat, although seen mostly as gold.

This breed is not recommended for first-time cat owners, since there are some common cat behaviors that the Munchkin is unable to do. Also, there is research looking to see if this mutation has, by chance, caused some other more severe genetic problems that have not become apparent.

The Munchkin, originally called the Creole Kangaroo because of its first arising in Louisiana, is known for its short basset-like legs that developed through a spontaneous mutation. Owned by Laurie Bobskill.

NORWEGIAN FOREST

This breed is to its home country what the Maine Coon is to the US. It is a tough cat that has been around in its native home for a few centuries so it is a no-frills, out-of-doors type of feline, the sort you see in many parts of Europe and America. A number of registers are now accepting the breed but the big ones, such as the CFA in the US and the GCCF in Britain do not. It looks similar to the Maine Coon but as stated it is a much older breed. You can have this breed in most colors other than pointed, chocolate or lilac. Given the range of available colors, we would assume that these have been introduced from other breeds over the years. It is a very nice cat but you will not have many opportunities of seeing them at this time.

Above: This brown ticked tabby Norwegian Forest displays the double coat that consists of a woolly undercoat. The coat is uneven—shorter on the shoulders and longer over the rest of the body. Owned by Dawn M. Shiley.

Right: The Norwegian Forest (Norsk Skaukatt), which originated in Scandinavia, is believed to have developed without any selective breeding by man. This brown tabby with white is just one of the many accepted colors. Owned by Bob and Linda Thaler.

The head of the Norwegian Forest should be triangular in shape and relatively large with large oval-shaped eyes. Eyes in shades of green and gold are accepted. Owned by Penny M. Kopf.

OCICAT

If you like spotted cats then the Ocicat is sure to be on your short list of breeds to check out. It is a large impressive breed that first turned up in a litter during 1964. The original kitten, called Tonga, was neutered and became a pet but further matings using the sire and dam commenced the breeding program of Virginia Daly, which has resulted in the present day breed.

The Ocicat gained acceptance with the CFA and TICA and its numbers have steadily swelled each year in terms of registrations. They are still not high but in percentage growth the breed is outperforming just about every other breed.

In appearance the Ocicat has a distinct wild look about it, which no doubt accounts for some of its appeal. It is neither cobby nor svelte, though clearly displaying its Abyssinian origins more than those of its Siamese ancestors. American Shorthairs also figured in its development in order to add size and colors to the breed. The result has been a happy union.

The Ocicat is a hybrid breed that developed through crossing the Abyssinian, American Shorthair, and Siamese. It has been named for the South American wild cat, the ocelot.

As if good looks were not enough, the breed is said to be very trainable and extremely affectionate. Indeed, this is one of its possible drawbacks for it does not like to be left alone, nor kept in confined surroundings.

The potential color range is very good and includes each of the obvious colors such as black, tawny (brown), blue, and lavender (lilac). Cinnamon is the term correctly used for those which appear red, but true red, which is sex- linked, cream and tortie are not acceptable in the breed. The colors are seen in the form of thumbprint shaped spots on a lighter agouti background. If you wish to see a lot of spots before your eyes then we feel you will be impressed by this breed.

The head of the Ocicat should be a wedgelike shape with moderately large almond-shaped eyes. The eyes should be slightly angled upward toward the ears.

The pattern of the Ocicat must have a tabby "M" on the forehead and markings over the head and between the ears. There must be spots scattered across the shoulders and hindquarters, and continuing down the legs.

OJOS AZULES

First discovered in New Mexico, the Ojos Azules' name comes from the Spanish, meaning "blue eyes," but the odd eyes are also

Ojos Azules, Spanish for "blue eyes," should have prominent, beautiful eyes. The eyes are the dominant feature of this breed and should be a nearly round almond shape.

accepted in this breed. All colors, categories and divisions are accepted in the Ojos Azules, and the pointed and particolors must have the white tip on the tail, that has also become one of the breed's hallmarks.

The body should be well proportioned, with the cat being of medium size, and the bones have been described as fine. Hind legs should be slightly angulated, thus they are slightly longer than the fore legs with relatively small feet. The Ojos Azules should have a supple and graceful appearance, with a tapering tail proportionate to the body size. The entire head should look as though the eyes are being displayed. In the triangular shape that is required in the breed, the eyes should appear prominent and dominate the entire head. It is the cat's "ojos" that should catch one's eye when studying the breed.

The Ojos Azules is a medium-sized cat that should appear graceful and well balanced. The breed is known for its sweet expression and lovely appearance. Owned by Laurie Bobskill.

The coat of this breed should be moderately short hair that is soft and silky. All colors and patterns are accepted as long as the blue eyes are present; the only coat color that is discouraged is solid white. Owned by Laurie Bobskill.

ORIENTAL SHORTHAIR

The Oriental Shorthair is best described as a Siamese of any color that is not accepted

The head must be a long wedge shape and have a flat skull, with almond-shaped eyes that are of moderate size. Green is the preferred eye color, although gold and copper are accepted.

under that breed's name. In the UK the latest standards show changes from the previous ones in the classification of what were Foreign Shorthairs. These are now divided between those of that name and the Oriental Shorthairs, which are largely the same as in the US except that the Havana and the Angora are grouped with the Orientals.

In appearance the Orientals are of the svelte Siamese body type with short glossy fur. The potential color and pattern range is vast and includes just about all possible combinations other than the pointed pattern of the Siamese. The first Orientals appeared as color mutations in the Siamese, same as the British breeders of the early 1950s developed the Havana. The breed gained recognition in the US during the 1970s and has enjoyed a steady increase in its numbers with each passing year.

The eye color of this breed should be green but in whites it may be blue in the US, while in the UK it must be blue. Odd eyed whites are not acceptable

The neck of the Oriental Shorthair should be very long and slender, and the hips should not be any wider than the shoulders. The legs are long and thin with the hind legs slightly longer than the front legs.

in either country. If you would like a Siamese but prefer to have this in a solid color or any other pattern than the pointed, then the Oriental will be the breed for you. If you live in the UK then the solid colors are simply called Foreign white, Foreign black and so on.

In the US, the Oriental Shorthair is a self-colored, shaded, smoke, or tabby Siamese. In the UK each self-color is recognized as a separate breed.

PERSIAN

Just about everyone is familiar with the Persian cat, not only because it is by far the most popular breed around the world, but because it is invariably the one chosen to advertise wool, rugs, and other items on the TV and in glossy magazines. In the UK it was known for a number of years simply as the Longhaired but now it is back to its former status and is called the Persian Longhair.

The immediate impression of the breed is of a cobby build with thick short legs, a round face, large paws and a medium to short tail. The whole of this superstructure is covered with a dense fur. This generous coat tends to make the cat look more massive than it actually is, though all Persians should be well-muscled.

The head should be round and massive thus having good width of skull. The forehead should be round and the cheeks full. The ears are short and rounded at their tips and

The Persian is the most popular breed in the world. They are believed to have descended from the Turkish Angora. This shaded silver Persian clearly shows the beauty of the breed.

must be well apart. The nose is short and wide with a stop or break. The chin is strong and rounded. The eyes should be round, and set well apart. The British standard says they must be bold and not deep set, while the American standard calls for their giving

the face a sweet expression. The neck should be short and thick.

The body should be of cobby type, low on the legs. The chest should be broad and deep while the shoulders and rump are to be massive and well-muscled. The mid body should be short and well-rounded. The legs are to be short, thick and strong with paws that are large, round, firm and preferably well tufted. The toes should be close. The correct tail will be short and carried below the level of the back. It should be bushy and proportionate to the body length. Overall, the Persian is a medium to large cat but quality is more important than size.

The coat is long, thick and of fine texture. The British standard calls for the fur not to be excessively woolly and it should be soft and full of life. The frill to be full and covering the shoulders and continuing

The head of the Persian should be broad and round with a sweet expression. The eyes must be large, round, and set far apart from each other, conforming to the coat color.

The Persian should be a well-balanced cat with excellent muscle tone. They are described as cobby and firm, of medium to large size.

into a deep frill between the front legs. The American standard (CFA) requires the fur to be long all over the body including the shoulders while the ruff is to be immense. Ear and toe tufts should be long.

Like many breeds or varieties in other pet species the Persian has reached a peak of perfection in many areas. This, combined with its immense popularity, is a mixed blessing. Once any breed attains a near ideal state then fashion tends to take over as there is nowhere for the breed to go in objectives. The result is that excess becomes the order of the day so in Persians the fur will get too long and too dense for comfort. The face becomes more foreshortened and will increase the number of problems with both dentition and with breathing. With the Peke-nosed Persian of the US the latter problem has already arrived. Unless associations (and judges) are somehow able to decide when enough is enough, then we

fear the Persian of the future will be a sad comparison to what it is today.

The Persian is available in just about every color and pattern of those known in cats. A few comments might be useful to those thinking of certain colors in the breed. The kittens in the pointed

breeds will not display this pattern well until they are mature so see as many of the breeder's stock and progeny as possible so you have a good idea how good the color and markings are.

The Persian is possibly the most domesticated breed of cat there is and this no doubt accounts for a good portion of its popularity. It is quite happy strolling round the home and following its owner wherever he or she goes. It is not an overly energetic cat compared to many breeds, another plus for many of its owners. It is very affectionate, it is elegant and you are spoiled about choice where color is concerned. It will require much grooming, for when Persians that have been neglected are seen they really are a sorry sight. Shop around for good kittens as there are a number of people breeding from inferior stock simply to cash in on the breed's immense popularity.

The Persian is known for its luxurious, long coat, which is soft and silky to the touch. The undercoat should be woolly and dense. The coat must be maintained on a daily basis to avoid matting.

RAGDOLL

The Ragdoll was first conceived and developed in California during the 1960s. It is not accepted by all US registries nor in Great Britain. It is a large cat with good length and muscle. The face is round and the ears are small to medium and set at an inclined angle and well apart. The coat is of medium length and silky, not unlike that of the Birman, so we will not present you with the problems of grooming associated with the Persian. The breed is noted for its gentle disposition, which is paramount in its qualities.

The breed is available in three colors which are colorpoint, mitted and bicolored. Each of these may be lilac (frost), blue, chocolate or seal. As nice as this breed is, we cannot help feeling it may suffer an identity problem which may hold back its popularity. This is a problem facing any relatively new breed that does not have a distinctive feature. If you are looking for a kitten that will grow to be quite good sized cat and should have a very placid temperament then you might find the Ragdoll worth considering.

The Ragdoll is available in three color varieties: colorpoint, mitted, and bicolored. The coat of the Ragdoll is longest around the neck and the face, and it should be brushed on a regular basis to keep it healthy looking.

The Ragdoll is a wonderfully docile animal that shows a lot of affection toward its owners. It is a large cat that can take up to three years to mature fully.

RUSSIAN BLUE

The Russian Blue has been recognized as a breed since the turn of the century, though it is thought to have existed for a few hundred years as a mutational color. The original cats were shipped to England from the port of Archangel, so it is no surprise to find it was called

The most outstanding characteristic of the Russian Blue is the double coat, which is silky, stands upright, and short. The coat should have silver-tipped guard hairs to contrast against the solid blue body color.

the Archangel cat. The first cats arrived in England during the 1880s and during that same period

were exported to the US.

The breed is one of the many that are neither cobby nor Siamese in terms of their conformation. They are lithe, elegant cats with good muscle. In the US only blue is permitted as a color but in the UK the Russian White and the Russian Black have preliminary status at this time. The coat is short, very glossy and dense. The preferred color in blues is medium and it should exhibit silver tipping. The quality and color of the coat is very important in this breed for it is the most outstanding single feature. The eye color should be a vivid green and the shape is that of an almond—this applies in the UK to both whites and blacks as well.

The Russian Blue is more popular than the Korat but has been around quite a bit longer. It is the most elegant of the blue breeds, has a wonderful personality and is well recommended. It is not a commonly seen breed so you may have to look a little bit further

The Russian Blue must have a modified wedge-shaped head, with upturned corners of the mouth to give the cat a smiling expression. The eyes should be as green as possible, and kittens' eyes will change from yellow to green.

afield to locate examples than with breeds such as Persians, or popular shorthairs.

The Russian Blue was believed to have come from Russia to the UK from a port called Archangelsk, thus the breed was called the Archangel cat for a short time.

SCOTTISH FOLD

The Scottish Fold originated as a mutation, in 1961, within farmyard cats owned by William and Mary Ross of Perthshire. Your kittens should therefore be able to trace their origins back to the original Fold cat, Susie. In all respects the breed should be regarded as a flop-eared British or American Shorthair, so these breeds can be referred to for more details. Essentially, this is a cobby cat with short, dense and glossy fur. The breed is not recognized in Great Britain as it is based on a genetic abnormality.

The ears fold forward to give the breed a very unusual, yet most attractive appearance. However, the mutant genes involved are also linked to physical problems if in the homozygous state. The result is that such cats may develop dysplasia, which affects the ball and socket hip joints and can result in the cat having difficulty in walking. It is a malady seen quite a lot in certain dog breeds, where it is always a major

The Scottish Fold first occurred as an ear mutation in some farm cats in Scotland. The breed was established by crossing the British Shorthair and various domestic cats of both Scotland and England.

problem. Other problems include a swelling of the paws and legs as well as undue thickening of the tail.

The breed is available in all colors and patterns with the exception of chocolate, lavender(lilac) and the Himalayan (Siamese) pattern, or these combinations with white. This is a nice breed were it not for the potential problems, which are sufficient for us to suggest considerable caution to the would-be purchaser.

The round head and well-padded body give the Scottish Fold the overall appearance of a medium-sized, well-rounded cat.

The head of the Scottish Fold is round and broad with a firm jaw and chin. The eyes are large and round, giving the cat a wonderfully sweet expression.

There is also the Long Haired Scottish Fold, which is a relatively recent addition to this breed. It has all the features of the breed along with longer hair covering the body.

SELKIRK REX

The Selkirk Rex, seen both in short hair and long hair, has been produced by a dominant gene that affected the guard, down and awn hairs, where the characteristic curl is seen the most around the neck and tail. The coat is dense and the down hairs seem slightly coarse to the touch. The coat is also arranged in individual curls. The Selkirk Rex is a medium to large cat that has gained weight due to the heavy

The head of the Selkirk Rex should be round with full cheeks. The whiskers must be curled, along with the rest of the coat. The squared off muzzle shows off the curled whiskers.

The torso of the Selkirk Rex should be well muscled and rectangular, and the legs should be medium-sized with good bone structure. Owned by Laurie Bobskill.

The Selkirk Rex occurred through a mutation that produced a curly effect on the guard, down, and awn hairs. The curl is most visible around the neck and tail. Owned by Laurie Bobskill.

boning of the skeleton. All colors are seen in this breed along with all categories and divisions.

The shape of the head is very round with full cheeks, and the muzzle is short with a nose stop to give the Selkirk Rex a unique profile. The eyes and ears are set apart with the ears being medium sized and pointed. The torso is very muscular with a rectangular shape, and the tail is medium size and quite thick.

SIAMESE

It is doubtful that any other breed of cat is quite as well known throughout the world as the Siamese. Its very individual markings and svelte body shape, together with an almost non cat-like personality, combine to make a quite unique breed. It has also been of great importance in the development of a number of other breeds.

The breed is strongly associated with the seal point color and it was a dark example of this that made its first appearance at the 1871 cat show held at Crystal Palace, London. It attracted much attention and soon others were being imported. These were not the lithe cats you will see today but more stocky examples, possibly not even good ones. The King of Siam (now Thailand) gave cats to his friends in both Britain and the US and these prob-ably helped improve the genetic material of the breed.

The blue point Siamese may have come about by a mutation within the breed, but it is known that the Russian Blue was used in many matings and this certainly spread the genes for the color. It was some years before blues were accepted and the same is true of the chocolate and its dilution, the lilac. In the US only these four colors are accepted as Siamese but in the UK there are tabby points, red points, torties points, creams and others. These are regarded as Oriental Shorthairs in the US.

In terms of its conformation the Siamese is a medium sized breed with a long svelte body supported on long slim legs. The head is wedge-shaped and the neck is long and slender. The ears are large, pointed and wide at their base. The eyes are

The Siamese should be a graceful cat of medium size with long tapering lines. The body is long with hard muscles and fine bone.

almond-shaped and should slant towards the nose. The tail is long, thin and tapering to a fine point. Evidence of a kink in the tail is a serious fault, as is a weak chin that produces an uneven bite. The eye color must be a clear, vivid blue and any other color is a major fault. The coat should be very short, fine in texture, close lying, and glossy.

The personality of a Siamese is very different to most breeds and is often compared to that of a dog as much as a cat. They are extremely affectionate, more trainable than many breeds and are obviously very intelligent. As a result they do require more attention than many breeds, and will not be happy if left alone for any length of time. The answer is of course to have two kittens, but when these are left alone they will possi-

The Colorpoint Shorthair is essentially a Siamese with points colored other than those recognized by most US cat registries.

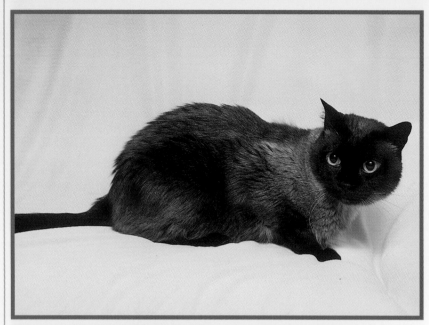

This is an old-style Siamese: it reflects the look of the breed as was popular several decades ago.

The coloring of the Siamese's short, fine coat is called pointed, meaning that the mask, ears, feet, and tail are clearly defined and consistently marked.

bly get up to a lot of mischief playing with each other, though this is preferable to a lonely Siamese. It is a breed well recommended to those who have the time to devote to them.

In recent years the breed has overcome many of the problems created by immense popularity but even so you should choose your supplier with care. If you plan to exhibit or breed your Siamese then check out the record of potential breeders in terms of the health and vigor of their stock before committing. This can be done not only by talking with people at major cat shows, but also by seeking advice from the nearest Siamese cat club to your locality.

Colorpoint Shorthairs possess the same alert, inquisitive nature as do their Siamese brother and sisters.

SIBERIAN

The Siberian is of Russian descent that somewhat resembles the Maine Coon, thus resembling the typical forest cat. These cats are large, strong cats that are known to be excellent leapers. Their muscles are impressive and stand out from the body, with a long slightly curved back. The hind legs are slightly longer than the fore legs, with round large paws.

When looking at the Siberian one notices strength and size and the excellent overall condition of the cat. The breed shows off its round shaped features along with a sweet face.

The coat is moderately long with certain areas, especially around the shoulder blades, thicker and of slightly shorter length. All colors and divisions are accepted, and there should be a ruff that sets off the large head. The Siberian has a modified wedge shaped head with rounded lines, and the skull is broad. The ears and the eyes are set pretty far apart from each other, and the eyes are round with no relationship between the coat color and their color. Lynx tipping on the ears is desirable, and there should be hair over the back of the ears.

The Siberian is a new breed in the US, but it is one of Russia's ancient pedigreed cats. Since arriving, the Siberian has made quite an impression on the cat world and hopefully will gain its deserved acclaim.

SINGAPURA

The Singapora is a relatively new breed that is recognized in the US by at least three associations, but is unknown in the UK. It is only the second breed which has agouti ticking as the pattern of its coat—the Abyssinian being the other. It is a small to medium sized breed that was imported from Singapore. It has a rounded head, large almond-shaped eyes and good sized ears. The tail is slender but with a blunt tip—not tapering as in the Siamese. The coat is very short, close lying to the body and glossy. A springy coat is a definite fault as are small eyes, barring on the tail, white lockets, unbroken necklaces or leg bracelets and lack of ticking on the head.

Presently just one color is recognized and this is a brown ticking on an ivory ground color. The hair tips should be the darkest color and at least one other band

The Singapura comes from the island nation of Singapore, where they roam as street cats. They are affectionate with the people they know best.

of ticking along the hair shaft is desired. The eye color may be hazel, green or yellow—any other is a serious fault.

To this point in time the breed has not made any great impact in the eight or

so years since it gained initial recognition but agouti patterned pets of any species rarely become very popular so this is only par for the course. It is an attractive breed that is sure to gather a dedicated group of enthusiasts to it.

The Singapura is a medium to small shorthaired cat whose endearing face is dominated by its large eyes and ears. The coat has an iridescent shading which gives the breed a look of refined and delicate coloring.

SNOWSHOE

The Snowshoe is even less established than the Singapora and at this time has only development status with a couple of American registries. It is a hybrid of the American Bi-Color Shorthair and the Siamese and presently is quite variable in type and color pattern. Nice examples are rather like shorthaired Ragdolls for they have white mittens and the dark points of a Siamese with a darker body color than in the latter breed.

Type will vary between those having a more Siamese look to them and those showing more American Shorthair. The coat lays close to the body and is very glossy. A potentially very pretty breed, nonetheless we feel it will have a hard struggle to become established due to the competition from the Ragdoll and from the much more established Birmans. Its personality should be very good and it will be an intelligent and hardy breed given its parent breeds.

The Snowshoe derived from a crossing of a Siamese and a bicolor American Shorthair. The dark points and white paws on this shorthaired cat set the breed apart from the rest.

SOMALI

The Somali is a longhaired Abyssinian which is thought to have appeared naturally in the breed during the 1960s, though at the time there were those who believed it was introduced from Persia. The length of the coat is not excessive so you would not be confronted with a major grooming problem. The tail is bushy and there should be a good density to the body fur, which should also be silky. A good ruff and breeches is preferred in the breed so as to

The regal Somali should be of medium size with defined musculature. They are active cats that show much interest in their surroundings.

The Somali is the longhaired version of the Abyssinian. It developed due to a spontaneous mutation, and it possesses the personality and charm of the Aby.

give the impression of a full coated cat. The ears may sport tufts. Refer to the Abyssinian for further details on the breed.

The Somali is available in the colors given for the Abyssinian, which in Great Britain comprise a more extensive list than in the US. However, such colors will no doubt also be accepted in due course in North America. The Somali is a very pretty cat that will appeal to those who like to see a little extra length of coat but not so much that it creates a grooming problem.

The coat is fine to the touch and only allowed in the tabby variety. The Somali should have a double coat, and the denser the coat, the better.

SPHYNX

This breed is based on the genetic abnormality for hairlessness. Actually, the Sphynx is not devoid of hair but for practical purposes it may be regarded as such. The mutation has appeared a number of times over the years and the present breed is based on one that occurred in Canada during 1966. Its body type is that of a foreign so it has a svelte body and looks rather like a rex breed minus the hair. It is variably described as cute, bizarre or horrible—depending on your views on how a cat should look.

Its personality is said to be super and there appears to be no negative side affects that are linked to the condition of hairlessness. It is available in just about any color or pattern and while this might sound strange, given the fact it has almost no hair, it is the skin that is colored.

The breed is not recognized

The Sphynx appears to be hairless, but in fact the body is covered with a fine coat that can barely be seen by the naked eye.

in Britain, nor is it ever likely to be, and the same is true for most American registries. For a while the Canadian registry recognized the breed but they later withdrew this. As the breed ages its skin will wrinkle and it is obviously prone to both sunburn and to cold weather. In a home that did not

give the breed special consideration it could lead a very unhappy life due to the effects of heat and cold. There is no merit in perpetuating breeds based on abnormalities, which might adversely affect the general well being of the cats themselves, so we cannot recommend this breed to would-be kitten owners.

The hairlessness of the Sphynx was the result of a spontaneous mutation that intrigued the cat world. After many years of controversy, breeders developed a hardy, genetically strong purebred cat.

The body of this breed should be slender with a well-rounded, thick abdomen that gives a pot-bellied appearance.

TONKINESE

This breed is the hybrid of the Burmese and the Siamese. It is recognized in four North American associations but not in Great Britain, though light-phase Burmese are sometimes referred to in that country as Tonkinese. The breed was developed in the US commencing in the 1960s and gained recognition during the late 1970s, since then its numbers have slowly increased.

This is a very pretty breed that is visually something between a Burmese and a Siamese, so it is svelte but not excessively so. The coat is short, silky and very glossy. The eye color is described as aqua and is an important feature of the breed.

Five colors are accepted and these equate those of the parents breeds plus one. Each is given the additional suffix of 'mink' and they are as follows: Natural mink is a medium brown shading to

The Tonkinese is a hybrid of the Siamese and the Burmese and presents the best features of each breed. Its body shape is a blend of the slender Siamese and the cobby Burmese.

dark brown on the points and equates the seal of Siamese or sable of the Burmese. Champagne mink is a dark cream shading to medium brown on the points and equates chocolate point in the Siamese and champagne in the Burmese. Platinum mink is a silvery gray shading to a darker pewter gray on the points. It equates the lilac point of the Siamese and the platinum of the Burmese. Blue mink is a soft blue shading to a darker slate blue and is the blue of the parent breeds. Honey mink is a golden or apricot

The Tonkinese is a confident cat with an outgoing personality that possesses the ability to communicate well with its family.

cream shading to a light to medium brown and genetically is a light champagne in which selection for the lightest examples has taken place.

The Tonkinese has a delightful personality and is a breed that will not be happy if left alone to its own devices for any length of time. Well recommended.

This mink Tonkinese shows the pointed coloring that was inherited from the Siamese.

TURKISH ANGORA

This very old breed is also known simply as Angora, depending on which association's standards you are reading. When Persian cats were originally imported into Europe the Angora was also seen in numbers, both being called Eastern cats or French cats (as many arrived straight nose. There is an obvious muzzle while the ears are large and pointed. The body is of medium size, lithe and graceful. The Angora is available in most colors and patterns though the Himalayan (Siamese) markings, lilac and chocolate are not acceptable in the US. The latter two colors are recognized in Great Britain.

The Turkish Angora is a perfectly balanced animal with a silky coat and a long muscular body.

The Turkish Angora was developed by the Tartars and the Chinese, who domesticated the Pallas cat. The breed was later perfected in Turkey.

In the US any tendency towards the Persian type body earns disqualification from exhibition. The Angora is a very beautiful and graceful breed that will appeal to those who like the more dainty longhaired cat.

in England from France). The texture of the fur of the Angora is smooth and silky, whereas that of the Persian is more woolly. It was the latter that ultimately become more fashionable because it could be made denser with selective breeding. The Angora thus drifted into obscurity but was still bred in its homeland.

During the 1950s the Angora started to appear again in Europe as well as in the US, where cats were imported direct from Turkey and from the nucleus of breeding cats kept at the Ankara Zoo. The pure Angora is a white cat (even those in the zoo program at Ankara) with no trace of any other colors and is a blue eyed breed. However, today the breed is seen in many colors.

In type it has a wedge shaped face with a long and

The Turkish Angora is an intelligent breed that is quite active and curious about its surroundings. It enjoys spending time with its family members.

Odd-eyed white Turkish Angora.

Although the Turkish Van is a very independent cat, it is still highly affectionate toward people.

TURKISH VAN

The Turkish Van breed is fully recognized in Britain but only by TICA in the US. Other US associations refer to the Van as a color variant of the Persian. The Turkish Van breed originates from the Lake Van area which lies between Russian Armenia and Iran (formerly Persia). The Van is clearly a variant of the Angora to which it is structurally very similar. The original Van cats were pure white but with auburn markings on the head, but not below the eyes. They should have auburn tails but these will show a faint ring pattern, which is more evident in kittens. This color may also be seen on the back in some individuals.

In Great Britain the cream Van now has preliminary status. It is a white cat with cream replacing the auburn. Faults in the breed are any tendency to display Siamese, Persian or British type, kinked or abnormal tails, squints and under or overshot jaws.

Being so similar to the Angora it will be a case of whether the color pattern appeals, this is the distinctive feature of a Turkish Van. In books, and the official standards, produced in Britain prior to 1988 you will find the breed simply called the Turkish.

The Turkish Angora shares a close heritage with the Turkish Van.

SUGGESTED READING

T.F.H. offers the most comprehensive selection of books dealing with cats. A selection of significant titles is presented below; they and many other works are available from your local pet shop.

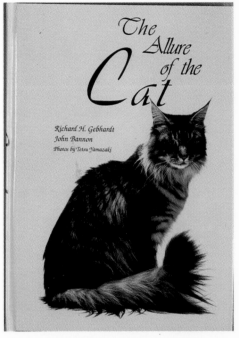

TS-173, 304 pages
over 400 full-color photos

TS-127, 384 pages
over 350 full-color photos

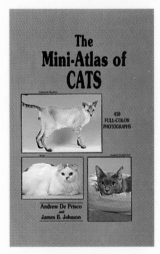

TS-152,
448 pages
over 400 full-
color photos

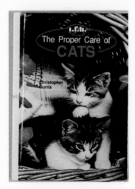

TW-103,
256 pages
over 200 full-
color photos

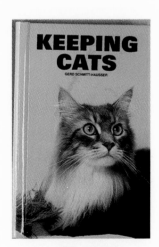

TS-219,
192 pages
over 90 full-
color photos

INDEX

Page numbers in **boldface** refer to illustrations.

Acknowledgment

This volume in the *Basic Domestic Pet Library* series was researched in part at the Ontario Veterinary college at the University of Guelph in Guelph, Ontario, and was published under the auspice of Dr. Herbert R. Axelrod.

A world-renown scientist, explorer, author, university professor, lecturer, and publisher, Dr. Axelrod is the best-known tropical fish expert in the world and the founder and chairman of T.F.H. Publications, Inc., the largest and most respected publisher of pet literature in the world. He has written 16 definitive texts on Ichthyology (including the bestselling *Handbook of Tropical Aquarium Fishes*), published more than 30 books on individual species of fish for the hobbyist, written hundreds of articles, and discovered hundreds of previously unknown species, six of which have been named after him.

Dr. Axelrod holds a Ph.D and was awarded an Honorary Doctor of Science degree by the University of Guelph, where he is now an adjunct professor in the Department of Zoology. He has served on the American Pet Products Manufacturers Association Board of Governors and is a member of the American Society of Herpetologists and Ichthyologists, the Biometric Society, the New York Zoological Society, the New York Academy of Sciences, the American Fisheries Society, the National Research Council, the National Academy of Sciences, and numerous aquarium societies around the world.

In 1977, Dr. Axelrod was awarded the Smithson Silver Medal for his ichthyological and charitable endeavors by the Smithsonian Institution. A decade later, he was elected an endowment member of the American Museum of Natural History and was named a life member of the James Smithson Society by the Smithsonian Associates' national board. He has donated in excess of $50 million in recent years to the American Museum of National History, the University of Guelph, and other institutions.